Guardian of the Redeemer

ANNIVERSARY EDITION

Guardian of the Redeemer

ANNIVERSARY EDITION

POPE JOHN PAUL II

With commentary by Dr. Joseph C. Atkinson

BOOKS & MEDIA
Boston

Library of Congress Cataloging-in-Publication Data

Catholic Church. Pope (1978-2005 : John Paul II)
  [Redemptoris custos. English]
  Guardian of the Redeemer / Saint Pope John Paul II ; with commentary
by Dr. Joseph C. Atkinson. -- Anniversary Edition.
      pages cm
  Includes bibliographical references.
  ISBN-13: 978-0-8198-3130-9
  ISBN-10: 0-8198-3130-1
  1. Joseph, Saint. I. John Paul II, Pope, 1920-2005. II. Title.
  BT690.C3813 2014
  232.9'32--dc23

                          2013036649

Cover design by Rosana Usselmann

Cover art by E. Murillo / background: © istockphoto.com

Published by Pauline Books & Media, 50 Saint Pauls Avenue, Boston, MA 02130–3491

Printed in the U.S.A.

www.pauline.org

Pauline Books & Media is the publishing house of the Daughters of St. Paul, an international congregation of women religious serving the Church with the communications media.

1 2 3 4 5 6 7 8 9   18 17 16 15 14

Contents

Preface

On the 100th anniversary of Leo XIII's encyclical on Saint Joseph, *Quamquam Pluries*, John Paul II decided to turn his gaze, and thereby the gaze of the whole Church, upon the guardian of Jesus, the spouse of Mary, and the patron of the universal Church. The pope's aim was to encourage all to grow in their devotion to Saint Joseph.

Saint Joseph's importance as husband and father was recognized from the very beginning of the Church and recorded in Scripture. Nonetheless, devotion to Saint Joseph followed a rather long and slow trajectory. Clearly Joseph played a key role in the initial preparation for the Incarnation. Yet he was taken officially into the heart of the Church's liturgical life only after centuries of theological development.

It was not until 1962, in fact, that John XXIII at Vatican Council II inserted Joseph's name into the Roman Canon of the Mass. While it appears that specific forms of devotion to Joseph developed in the early centuries of the Coptic Church (and were often associated with the flight into Egypt), it was not until the Middle Ages that a cult of Saint Joseph began in the West. In 1359 Saint Joseph's name was added to the Litany of Saints, but it was omitted during the Tridentine reforms of the sixteenth century and restored again in 1726. The first indulgenced novena to Saint Joseph was approved in 1713 by Clement XI, yet it was not until 1909 that Pius X give formal approval to a public litany of Saint Joseph.[*]

This slow theological development culminated in the nineteenth and twentieth centuries when the foundational truths of Scripture and the centuries-old theological intuitions concerning Saint Joseph finally coalesced. In 1870, Pius IX declared Saint Joseph to be the patron of the Catholic Church. Then, in 1899, Leo XIII supplemented Pius's initiative by issuing *Quamquam Pluries* to encourage the Christian people to invoke Saint Joseph, trusting in his intercession. At the time, morals and faith were degenerating, and so the pope urged that "devotion to Saint Joseph should engraft itself upon the daily pious practices of Catholics" (*QP* 2).

God always provides what is most needed for the good of the Church. Why then has Joseph become so prominent in the Church's awareness in this modern period? Perhaps the answer is that opposition to the faith today centers primarily on the family. It is being attacked in an unprecedented manner by many who wish to deform and destroy it (see *Familiaris Consortio* 3). Today human life has only accidental

---

[*] See *Saint Joseph in the Liturgy* at www.osjoseph.org/stjoseph/liturgy/partB.php. Here, the Oblates of Saint Joseph provide a helpful comprehensive history of Saint Joseph.

value, sexuality is a human or government construct, and chastity is scorned. Yet, even within the darkness of our own times, there are signs of hope as people begin to seek to discover God's will for marriage and family.

In many ways our culture is like the world culture of Jesus's time. He was born into a world dominated by paganism and violence. God commanded Joseph, the head of the Holy Family, to bring to safety "his precious treasures" (*RC* 1) Jesus and Mary. Now, as the Church is again surrounded by a destructive culture, she turns in prayer to Christ and invokes the protection and powerful intercession of Saint Joseph.[*]

John Paul II's apostolic exhortation *Redemptoris Custos* theologically strengthened recovery of the value of Joseph. In this work, the Holy Father reveals the inner logic of Saint Joseph's interior life and vocation. While his entire being was permeated by silence (we have no recorded words of Joseph), John Paul II saw this contemplative silence as the foundation for Joseph's entire life.

The unique contribution John Paul II makes in this document is his emphasis on the *realism* of Joseph and Mary's marriage. In Catholic theology there is no room for dualism, which views the body and the soul in opposition to each other. For human persons both the body and the spirit are essential, yet they are configured in a specific

---

[*] Interestingly, in May 2013, Pope Francis wanted to intentionally turn the gaze of the Church upon the *fatherly* care of Joseph by inserting Saint Joseph's name into three more canons of the Mass.

manner. John Paul II *boldly* states that it is as important for the Church to uphold the reality of Joseph and Mary's marriage as it is to profess the virginal conception of Jesus (*RC* 7). Unflinchingly, the Holy Father addresses the seeming impossibility for virginity and real conjugal love to co-exist in their marriage. He carefully unpacks the paradox here and shows how these mutually exclusive loves can, in fact, be united in one who is sanctified. Virginity and conjugal love are thus intrinsically related. On this basis, John Paul II demonstrates how by the Spirit conjugal love is perfected in Saint Joseph. Joseph is not less a father or a husband, rather he actually realizes the full meaning of both through the total gift of self.

Given the current crisis of the family and fatherhood, it seems providential that such a humble and just figure be raised up for our consideration. Joseph models for us what it is to be a just man, a holy husband, and a faithful father, one who can intercede powerfully for us and for the Church.

Topical Outline

APOSTOLIC EXHORTATION OF THE
SUPREME PONTIFF JOHN PAUL II

Guardian of the Redeemer

Redemptoris Custos

On the Person and Mission of Saint Joseph
in the Life of Christ and of the Church

To Bishops, to Priests and Deacons, to Men and Women
Religious, and to all the Lay Faithful

Introduction

1. "Joseph did *as the angel of the Lord commanded him and took his wife*" (cf. Mt 1:24).

Inspired by the Gospel, the Fathers of the Church from the earliest centuries stressed that just as Saint Joseph took loving care of Mary and gladly dedicated himself to Jesus Christ's upbringing,[1] he likewise watches over and protects Christ's Mystical Body, that is, the Church, of which the Virgin Mary is the exemplar and model.

On the occasion of the centenary of Pope Leo XIII's Encyclical Epistle *Quamquam Pluries*,[2] and in line with the veneration given to Saint Joseph over the centuries, I wish to offer for your consideration, dear brothers and sisters, some reflections concerning him "into whose custody God entrusted his most precious treasures."[3] I gladly fulfill this pastoral duty so that all may grow in devotion to the Patron of the Universal Church and in love for the Savior whom he served in such an exemplary manner.

In this way the whole Christian people not only will turn to Saint Joseph with greater fervor and invoke his patronage with trust, but also will always keep before their eyes his

1

humble, mature way of serving and of "taking part" in the plan of salvation.[4]

I am convinced that by reflection upon the way that Mary's spouse shared in the divine mystery, the Church—on the road toward the future with all of humanity—will be enabled to discover ever anew her own identity within this redemptive plan, *which is founded on the mystery of the Incarnation.*

This is precisely the mystery in which Joseph of Nazareth "shared" like no other human being except Mary, the Mother of the Incarnate Word. He shared in it with her; he was involved in the same salvific event; he was the guardian of the same love, through the power of which the eternal Father "destined us to be his sons through Jesus Christ" (Eph 1:5).

Ponder

Why should we focus on Saint Joseph? The answer given by the Church, which John Paul II affirms, is that God *entrusted* his most precious treasures to this humble carpenter. Jesus, the Son of God, and Mary, the immaculate mother of the Christ, were given into Joseph's care (see *RC* 1 and footnote 4). If God trusts Joseph with responsibility for Jesus and Mary, we too can confidently entrust ourselves to his intercession and patronage.

In our modern age, it sounds odd to speak of someone being a patron of someone else. This goes against the spirit of today's world, which believes everyone is an autonomous individual. But the Scriptures show us that salvation is always both personal and corporate. God alone is the source of our salvation but, in respecting the freedom he gave us, the Lord invites us to cooperate with him. Jesus does not simply show up in human history. Rather, Mary and Joseph cooperate with the Father to bring into the world the very cause of our salvation, Jesus, and to protect and nourish him.

In this exhortation, John Paul II links devotion to Saint Joseph with our love for Jesus, thereby showing the Christological foundation of devotion to this saint. We are to grow "in love for the Savior whom he [Joseph] served" (*RC* 1). Devotion to Saint Joseph ultimately springs from a love of Jesus himself. As we grow in devotion to Joseph we will find that he, like Mary, always points us to Jesus, "whom he served."

Joseph fulfills a twofold ministry to the People of God. First, he is an *intercessor* for us, a powerful intercessor whom we can trust. If God entrusts so much to him, so can we. We can ask him to be our patron, to accompany us on our pilgrimage through life, and to intercede with God on our behalf. Second, he is a preeminent *model* for all Christians. By his life, Joseph gives us the example of how a person takes part in salvation (*RC* 1). He shows us how to "work out . . . [our] salvation" (Phil 2:12) with both humility and maturity.

Saint Joseph is not only a model for the individual Christian, but also for the Church itself. No other human being, besides Mary, shared so deeply in the divine mystery of Jesus becoming man. Consequently, John Paul II is convinced that as the Church reflects on how Joseph "shared in the divine mystery" (*RC* 1), she will also be able to rediscover her own identity within that plan. What Joseph did, the Church is called to do: be humble, be open to God, and be the guardian of the divine life in this world.

1. The saints are fellow Christians who have been perfected by the love of Jesus. The Book of Revelation speaks of the "bowls filled with incense, which are the prayers of the holy ones" (Rev 5:8). Because of their love for Jesus, the saints intercede for us before our heavenly Father. What do I know about the Communion of Saints? How can I cultivate love for the saints and strengthen my relationship with them?

2. Other than Mary, no one experienced the mystery of the Incarnation as profoundly as Joseph did. The fragility of the divine infant life was handed over to him to care for, protect, and guide. What must it have been like for Joseph to take on the role of father to the Son of God? How must he have felt and dealt with these emotions?

3. Joseph played a specific role in salvation history. The Church has affirmed that God entrusted "his most precious treasures" to him. Do I see myself as having a vocation within the body of Christ or do I see my spiritual life as just something personal? How can I discover the vocation God has planned for me? How can I live my vocational commitment with greater love?

Pray

Father, in love you created us and redeemed us. In love you make us a part of the body of your Son, so that now we never have to live in isolation from you or from one other. Thank you for the Communion of Saints, our fellow Christians who have gone before us, perfected by the love of Christ. In particular, help us come to know the foster father of your Son, Saint Joseph. Knowing that you entrusted to him your most precious treasures, Jesus and Mary, may we have ever greater confidence in his intercession for us. Amen.

Act

Read books or visit Catholic websites (e.g., www.osjo seph.org) that deal with the life of Saint Joseph so you can become more familiar with him and his role in salvation history.

PART I

The Gospel Portrait

Marriage to Mary

2. "Joseph, Son of David, *do not fear to take Mary* your wife, for that which is conceived in her is of the Holy Spirit; she will bear a son, and you shall call his name Jesus, for he will save his people from their sins" (Mt 1:20–21).

In these words we find the core of biblical truth about Saint Joseph; they refer to that moment in his life to which the Fathers of the Church make special reference.

The evangelist Matthew explains the significance of this moment while also describing how Joseph lived it. However, in order to understand fully both its content and context, it is important to keep in mind the parallel passage in the *Gospel of Luke*. In Matthew we read: "Now the birth of Jesus Christ took place in this way. When his mother Mary had been betrothed to Joseph, before they came together she was found to be with child of the Holy Spirit" (Mt 1:18). However, the origin of Mary's pregnancy "of the Holy Spirit" is described more fully and explicitly in *what Luke tells us about the annunciation of Jesus' birth*: "The angel Gabriel was sent from God to a city of Galilee named Nazareth, to a virgin betrothed to a man whose name was Joseph, of the house of David; and the virgin's name was Mary" (Lk 1:26–27). The angel's greeting: "Hail, full of grace, the Lord is with you" (Lk 1:28), created an inner turmoil in Mary and also moved her to reflect. Then the messenger reassured the Virgin and at the same time revealed God's special plan for her: *"Do not be afraid, Mary, for you have found favor with God. And behold, you will conceive in your womb and bear a son*, and you shall call his name Jesus. He will be great, and will be called the Son of the Most High; and the Lord God will give to him the throne of his father David" (Lk 1:30–32).

A little earlier the Gospel writer had stated that at the moment of the annunciation, Mary was "betrothed to a man whose name was Joseph, of the house of David." The nature of this *"marriage"* is explained indirectly when Mary, after hearing what the messenger says about the birth of the child, asks, "How can this be, *since I do not know man?*" (Lk 1:34) The angel responds: "The Holy Spirit will come upon you, and the power of the Most High will overshadow you; therefore the child to be born will be called holy, the Son of God" (Lk 1:35). Although Mary is already "wedded" to Joseph, she will remain a virgin, because the child conceived in her at the annunciation was conceived by the power of the Holy Spirit.

At this point Luke's text coincides with Matthew 1:18 and serves to explain what we read there. If, after her marriage to Joseph, Mary "is found to be with child of the Holy Spirit," this fact corresponds to all that the annunciation means, in particular to Mary's final words: *"Let it be to me according to your word"* (Lk 1:38). In response to what is clearly the plan of God, with the passing of days and weeks Mary's "pregnancy" is visible to the people and to Joseph; she appears before them as one who must give birth and carry within herself the mystery of motherhood.

3. In these circumstances, "her husband Joseph, being a just man and unwilling to put her to shame, *resolved to send her away quietly*" (Mt 1:19). He did not know how to deal with Mary's "astonishing" motherhood. He certainly sought an answer to this unsettling question, but above all he sought a way out of what was for him a difficult situation. *"But as he considered this*, behold, an angel of the Lord appeared to him in a dream, saying, *Joseph*, son of David, *do not fear to take Mary your wife*, for that which is conceived in her is of the Holy Spirit; she will bear a son, and you shall call his name Jesus, for he will save his people from their sins'" (Mt 1:20–21).

There is a strict parallel between the "annunciation" in Matthew's text and the one in Luke. *The divine messenger introduces Joseph to the mystery of Mary's motherhood.* While remaining a virgin, she who by law is his "spouse" has become a mother through the power of the Holy Spirit. And when the Son in Mary's womb comes into the world, he must receive the name Jesus. This was a name known among the Israelites and sometimes given to their sons. In this case, however, *it is the Son who*, in accordance with the divine promise, *will bring to perfect fulfillment the meaning of the name Jesus*—Yehos̆ ua'—which means *"God saves."*

Joseph is visited by *the messenger* as "Mary's spouse," as the one who in due time must give this name to the Son to be born of the Virgin of Nazareth who is married to him. It is *to Joseph,* then, that the messenger turns, *entrusting to him the responsibilities of an earthly father with regard to Mary's Son.*

"When Joseph woke from sleep, he did as the angel of the Lord commanded him and took Mary as his wife" (cf. Mt 1:24). He took her in all the mystery of her motherhood. He took her together with the Son who had come into the world by the power of the Holy Spirit. In this way *he showed a readiness of will like Mary's* with regard to what God asked of him through the angel.

PONDER

At the heart of the mystery of Saint Joseph is his relationship to Mary, through which he enters into the mystery of the Incarnation. John Paul II thus begins his reflection by examining Joseph's marriage to Mary. This provides the background for Joseph's own form of an "annunciation" as recounted in Matthew 1:18–25 (*RC* 3). Like Mary, Joseph faced a moment of decision that would determine the whole course of his life. For Mary this seemingly came in a moment of quiet. For Joseph, this moment of decision came in a way that caused great agitation because the woman he was betrothed to was found with child.

In ancient Israel, one became legally betrothed first, then later married with the right to marital relations. Both states were legally binding. As a pious Jew, Joseph would have wanted to marry a virgin to protect his family lineage, but Mary appeared to have compromised her state. The Gospels make it clear that Joseph was not the father of the child. He then had to decide how he would live this moment of his life.

Here Joseph's character became a determining factor. The Gospel states that he was both a *just* man and *unwilling* to put her to shame (see Mt 1:19). Feeling shame himself because of the seeming betrayal, Joseph did not seek revenge. Rather, his love for Mary held firm and he resolved to send her away (Scripture uses the Hebrew term for divorce) quietly. As John Paul II notes, Joseph did not know how to deal with Mary's "astonishing" motherhood (*RC* 3). However, motivated by love, he sought a quiet way to resolve the situation.

Into this perplexing and bewildering context God entered and did what is seemingly impossible. He assured Joseph that Mary was still a virgin. Joseph was commanded not to fear to take Mary as his wife and to give the child the name of Jesus. Yet this still must have been mystifying. How could a woman be pregnant without "knowing" a man? Besides, what could it mean that this child was to save people from their sins? Who was this child? How could he possibly take away sins?

All of this profoundly challenged the landscape of Joseph's thought-world. He was asked to believe the impossible: that a child could be born of a virgin and could take away the sins of the world. At that point, this just man simply accepted the word of God. Like Mary, like Abraham, he trusted in the Lord. By accepting this word, he accepted the whole path of life that would flow from it. In obedience to God, Joseph named the child. By so doing he took upon himself the role of father with all its responsibilities. The bond of fatherhood, which was not his biologically, was replaced with the bond of paternity, which was his spiritually. Joseph's very openness to God allowed him to enter deeply into the mystery of salvation and enabled him to play his part.

1. Joseph faced a dilemma. To marry a pregnant woman would bring shame on the family and endanger the purity of the family line. Yet, motivated by justice and mercy, he did not want to bring shame on Mary. This was an impossible situation. How was it resolved? What steps did Joseph first take? What happened next? How do you usually react when you must face a crisis or difficult situation? How can you open yourself to God during these times?

2. Joseph faced a critical moment when he could either take a risk and follow God's words, or he could play it safe and refuse God's plan for his life. Think of times when you sensed God was calling you to do something. How did you respond? Are you more able to respond positively to God today? How do you listen for the word God sends to direct your life? What can you do to be more open to hearing God speak to you?

3. Joseph was faced with seeming infidelity. He knew Mary's character and could only feel bewildered over her "astonishing" motherhood, as John Paul II notes (*RC* 3). In this context, Joseph acted justly and lovingly because of his character and virtues. Then God intervened. How am I seeking to become a more virtuous person? In what ways am I cooperating with God to form and shape my character? (A good indication of this is how frequently I participate in the sacrament of Reconciliation.)

Pray

Father, you have given us the example of Abraham, Mary, and Joseph as people who hear a seemingly impossible word from you and yet believe. By trusting in you, they have helped to bring about the kingdom of God on earth. Give me the faith of Abraham so that I may believe even when I am old and outwardly useless; give me the faith of Mary so that I may trust even when following you may bring shame; and give me the faith of Joseph so that I may put my hand in yours and have utter confidence in you. Like them, may I say, "May it be done according to your word." Amen.

Act

The next time you are in a situation where you feel confused, bewildered, or betrayed, pause in the midst of your angst and think of Saint Joseph and his response to Mary. Ask Saint Joseph to intercede for you, that you might experience calm and be able to trust that God will work everything out for the good.

PART II

The Guardian of the Mystery of God

The Faith of Mary and Joseph

4. When, soon after the annunciation, Mary went to the house of Zechariah to visit her kinswoman Elizabeth, even as she offered her greeting she heard the words of Elizabeth, who was "filled with the Holy Spirit" (Lk 1:41). Besides offering a salutation which recalled that of the angel at the annunciation, Elizabeth also said: *"And blessed is she who believed that there would be a fulfillment of what was spoken to her from the Lord"* (Lk 1:45). These words were the guiding thought of the Encyclical *Redemptoris Mater*, in which I sought to deepen the teaching of the Second Vatican Council, which stated: "*the Blessed Virgin advanced in her pilgrimage of faith*, and faithfully preserved her union with her Son even to the cross,"[5] "preceding"[6] all those who follow Christ by faith.

Now at the beginning of this pilgrimage, *the faith of Mary meets the faith of Joseph*. If Elizabeth said of the Redeemer's

Mother, "blessed is she who believed," in a certain sense this blessedness can be referred to Joseph as well, since he responded positively to the word of God when it was communicated to him at the decisive moment. While it is true that Joseph did not respond to the angel's "announcement" in the same way as Mary, he "*did* as the angel of the Lord commanded him and took his wife." *What he did is the clearest "obedience of faith"* (cf. Rom 1:5, 16:26; 2 Cor 10:5–6).

One can say that *what Joseph did* united him in an altogether special way to the faith of Mary. *He accepted* as truth coming from God *the very thing* that *she had already accepted* at the annunciation. The Council teaches: "'The obedience of faith' must be given to God as he reveals himself. By this obedience of faith man freely commits himself entirely to God, making 'the full submission of his intellect and will to God who reveals,' and willingly assenting to the revelation given by him."[7] *This statement,* which touches the very essence of faith, *is perfectly applicable to Joseph of Nazareth.*

5. Therefore he became *a unique guardian of the mystery* "hidden for ages in God" (Eph 3:9), as did Mary, in that decisive moment which Saint Paul calls *"the fullness of time,"* when "God sent forth his Son, born of woman . . . to redeem those who were under the law, so that we might receive adoption as sons" (Gal 4:4–5). In the words of the Council: "It pleased God, in his goodness and wisdom, to reveal himself and to make known the mystery of his will (cf. Eph 1:9). His will was that men should have access to the Father, through Christ, the Word made flesh, in the Holy Spirit, and become sharers in the divine nature (cf. Eph 2:18; 2 Pt 1:4)."[8]

Together with Mary, Joseph is the first guardian of this divine mystery. Together with Mary, and in relation to Mary, *he shares in this final phase of God's self-revelation in Christ*, and he does so from the very beginning. Looking at the Gospel texts of both Matthew and Luke, one can also say that Joseph is the first *to share in the faith of the Mother of God* and that in doing so he supports his spouse in the faith of the divine annunciation. He is also the first to be placed by God on the path of Mary's "pilgrimage of faith." It is a path along which—especially at the time of Calvary and Pentecost—Mary will precede in a perfect way.[9]

6. The path that was Joseph's—*his pilgrimage of faith—ended first*, that is to say, before Mary stood at the foot of the cross on Golgotha, and before the time after Christ returned to the Father, when she was present in the upper room on Pentecost, the day the Church was manifested to the world, having been born in the power of the Spirit of truth. Nevertheless, *Joseph's way of faith moved in the same direction*: it was totally determined by the same mystery, of which he, together with Mary, had been the first guardian. The Incarnation and redemption constitute an organic and indissoluble unity, in which "the plan of revelation is realized by words and deeds which are intrinsically bound up with each other."[10] Precisely because of this unity, Pope John XXIII, who had a great devotion to Saint Joseph, directed that Joseph's name be inserted in the Roman Canon of the Mass—which is the perpetual memorial of redemption—after the name of Mary and before the apostles, popes, and martyrs.[11]

The Service of Fatherhood

7. As can be deduced from the Gospel texts, Joseph's marriage to Mary is the juridical basis of his fatherhood. It was to assure fatherly protection for Jesus that God chose Joseph to be Mary's spouse. It follows that Joseph's fatherhood—a relationship that places him as close as possible to Christ, to whom every election and predestination is ordered (cf. Rom 8:28–29)—comes to pass through marriage to Mary, that is, through the family.

While clearly affirming that Jesus was conceived by the power of the Holy Spirit, and that virginity remained intact in the marriage (cf. Mt 1:18–25; Lk 1:26–38), the evangelists refer to Joseph as Mary's husband and to Mary as his wife (cf. Mt 1:16, 18–20, 24; Lk 1:27; 2:5).

And while it is important for the Church to profess *the virginal conception of Jesus*, it is no less important to uphold *Mary's marriage to Joseph*, because juridically Joseph's fatherhood depends on it. Thus one understands why the generations are listed according to the genealogy of Joseph: "Why," Saint Augustine asks, "should they not be according to Joseph? Was he not Mary's husband? . . . Scripture states, through the authority of an angel, that he was her husband. *Do not fear*, says the angel, *to take Mary your wife, for that which is conceived in her is of the Holy Spirit.* Joseph was told to name the child, although not born from his seed. She *will bear a son*, the angel says, and *you will call him Jesus. Scripture recognizes that Jesus is not born of Joseph's seed, since in his concern about the origin of Mary's pregnancy, Joseph is told that it is of the Holy Spirit.* Nonetheless, he is not deprived of his fatherly authority from the moment that he is told to name the child. Finally, even the Virgin Mary, well aware that she has not conceived Christ as a result of conjugal relations with Joseph, still calls him *Christ's father.*"[12]

The *son of Mary* is also *Joseph's son* by virtue of the marriage bond that unites them: "By reason of their faithful marriage *both of them* deserve to be called Christ's parents, not only his mother, but also his father, who was a parent in the same way that he was the mother's spouse: *in mind*, not in the flesh."[13] In this marriage none of the requisites of marriage were lacking: "In Christ's parents all the goods of marriage were realized—offspring, fidelity, the sacrament: the *offspring* being the Lord Jesus himself; *fidelity*, since there was no adultery; the *sacrament*, since there was no divorce."[14]

Analyzing the nature of marriage, both Saint Augustine and Saint Thomas always identify it with an "indivisible union of souls," a "union of hearts," with "consent."[15] These elements are found in an exemplary manner in the marriage of Mary and Joseph. At the culmination of the history of salvation, when God reveals his love for humanity through the gift of the Word, it is precisely *the marriage of Mary and Joseph* that brings to realization in full "freedom" the "spousal gift of self" in receiving and expressing such a love.[16] "In this great undertaking which is the renewal of all things in Christ, marriage—it too purified and renewed—becomes a new reality, a sacrament of the New Covenant. We see that at the beginning of the New Testament, as at the beginning of the

Old, there is a married couple. But whereas Adam and Eve were the source of evil which was unleashed on the world, Joseph and Mary are the summit from which holiness spreads all over the earth. The Savior began the work of salvation by this virginal and holy union, wherein is manifested his all-powerful will to *purify and sanctify the family*—that sanctuary of love and cradle of life."[17]

How much the family of today can learn from this! "The essence and role of the family are, in the final analysis, specified by love. Hence the family has *the mission to guard, reveal, and communicate love*, and this is a living reflection of and a real sharing in God's love for humanity and the love of Christ the Lord for the Church his bride."[18] This being the case, it is in the Holy Family, the original "Church in miniature *(Ecclesia domestica)*,"[19] that every Christian family must be reflected. "Through God's mysterious design, it was in that family that the Son of God spent long years of a hidden life. It is therefore the prototype and example for all Christian families."[20]

8. Saint Joseph was called by God to serve the person and mission of Jesus directly *through the exercise of his fatherhood*. It is precisely in this way that, as the Church's liturgy teaches, he "cooperated in the fullness of time in the great mystery of salvation" and is truly a "minister of salvation."[21] His fatherhood is expressed concretely "in his having made his life a service, a sacrifice to the mystery of the Incarnation and to the redemptive mission connected with it; in having used the legal authority which was his over the Holy Family in order to make a total gift of self, of his life and work; in

having turned his human vocation to domestic love into a superhuman oblation of self, an oblation of his heart and all his abilities into love placed at the service of the Messiah growing up in his house."[22]

In recalling that "the beginnings of our redemption" were entrusted "to the faithful care of Joseph,"[23] the liturgy specifies that "God placed him at the head of his family, as a faithful and prudent servant, so that with fatherly care he might watch over his only begotten Son."[24] Leo XIII emphasized the sublime nature of this mission: "He among all stands out in his august dignity, since by divine disposition he was guardian, and according to human opinion, father of God's Son. Whence it followed that the Word of God was subjected to Joseph, he obeyed him and rendered to him that honor and reverence that children owe to their father."[25]

Since it is inconceivable that such a sublime task would not be matched by the necessary qualities to adequately fulfill it, we must recognize that Joseph showed Jesus "by a special gift from heaven, all the natural love, all the affectionate solicitude that a father's heart can know."[26]

Besides fatherly authority over Jesus, God also gave Joseph a share in the corresponding love, the love that has its origin in the Father "from whom every family in heaven and on earth is named" (Eph 3:15).

The Gospels clearly describe the fatherly responsibility of Joseph toward Jesus. For salvation—which comes through the humanity of Jesus—is realized in actions which are an everyday part of family life, in keeping with that "condescension" which is inherent in the economy of the Incarnation. The Gospel writers carefully show how in the life of Jesus nothing was left to chance, but how everything took place according to God's predetermined plan. The oft-repeated formula, "This happened, so that there might be fulfilled . . . ," in reference to a particular event in the Old Testament serves to emphasize the unity and continuity of the plan which is fulfilled in Christ.

With the Incarnation, the "promises" and "figures" of the Old Testament become "reality": places, persons, events, and rites interrelate according to precise divine commands communicated by angels and received by creatures who are particularly sensitive to the voice of God. Mary is the Lord's humble servant, prepared from eternity for the task of being the Mother of God. Joseph is the one whom God chose to be the "overseer of the Lord's birth,"[27] the one who has the responsibility to look after the Son of God's "ordained" entry into the world, in accordance with divine dispositions and human laws. All of the so-called "private" or "hidden" life of Jesus is entrusted to Joseph's guardianship.

The Census

9. Journeying to Bethlehem for the census in obedience to the orders of legitimate authority, Joseph fulfilled for the child the significant task of officially inserting the name "Jesus, son of Joseph of Nazareth" (cf. Jn 1:45) in the registry of the Roman Empire. This registration clearly shows that Jesus belongs to the human race as a man among men, a citizen of this world, subject to laws and civil institutions, but

also *"savior of the world."* Origen gives a good description of the theological significance, by no means marginal, of this historical fact: "Since the first census of the whole world took place under Caesar Augustus, and among all the others Joseph too went to register together with Mary his wife, who was with child, and since Jesus was born before the census was completed: to the person who makes a careful examination it will appear that a kind of mystery is expressed in the fact that at the time when all people in the world presented themselves to be counted, Christ too should be counted. By being registered with everyone, he could sanctify everyone; inscribed with the whole world in the census, he offered to the world communion with himself, and after presenting himself he wrote all the people of the world in the book of the living, so that as many as believed in him could then be written in heaven with the saints of God, to whom be glory and power for ever and ever, amen."[28]

The Birth at Bethlehem

10. As guardian of the mystery "hidden for ages in the mind of God," which begins to unfold before his eyes "in the fullness of time," *Joseph, together with Mary*, is a privileged witness to the birth of the Son of God into the world *on Christmas night in Bethlehem*. Luke writes: *"And while they were there, the time came for her to be delivered. And she gave birth to her firstborn son* and wrapped him in swaddling cloths, and laid him in a manger, because there was no place for them in the inn" (Lk 2:6–7).

Joseph was an eyewitness to this birth, which took place in conditions that, humanly speaking, were embarrassing —a first announcement of that "self-emptying" (cf. Phil 2:5–8) which Christ freely accepted for the forgiveness of sins. Joseph also *witnessed the adoration of the shepherds* who arrived at Jesus's birthplace after the angel had brought them the great and happy news (cf. Lk 2:15–16). Later he also *witnessed the homage of the magi who came from the East* (cf. Mt 2:11).

The Circumcision

11. A son's circumcision was the first religious obligation of a father, and with this ceremony (cf. Lk 2:21) Joseph exercised his right and duty with regard to Jesus.

The principle which holds that all the rites of the Old Testament are a shadow of the reality (cf. Heb 9:9ff.; 10:1) serves to explain why Jesus would accept them. As with all the other rites, circumcision too is "fulfilled" in Jesus. God's covenant with Abraham, of which circumcision was the sign (cf. Gn 17:13), reaches its full effect and perfect realization in Jesus, who is the "yes" of all the ancient promises (cf. 2 Cor 1:20).

Conferral of the Name

12. At the circumcision Joseph names the child "Jesus." This is the only name in which there is salvation (cf. Acts

4:12). Its significance had been revealed to Joseph at the moment of his "annunciation": "You shall call the child Jesus, for he will save his people from their sins" (cf. Mt 1:21). In conferring the name, Joseph declares his own legal fatherhood over Jesus, and in speaking the name he proclaims the child's mission as Savior.

The Presentation of Jesus in the Temple

13. This rite, to which Luke refers (2:22ff.), includes the ransom of the firstborn and sheds light on the subsequent stay of Jesus in the Temple at the age of twelve.

The ransoming of the firstborn is another obligation of the father, and it is fulfilled by Joseph. Represented in the firstborn is the people of the covenant, ransomed from slavery in order to belong to God. Here too, Jesus—who is the true "price" of ransom (cf. 1 Cor 6:20, 7:23; 1 Pt 1:19)—not only "fulfills" the Old Testament rite, but at the same time transcends it, since he is not a subject to be redeemed, but the very author of redemption.

The Gospel writer notes that "his father and his mother marveled at what was said about him" (Lk 2:23), in particular at *what Simeon said* in his canticle to God, when he referred to Jesus as the "salvation which you have prepared in the presence of all peoples, a light for revelation to the Gentiles, and for glory to your people Israel," and as a "sign that is spoken against" (cf. Lk 2:30–34).

The Flight into Egypt

14. After the presentation in the Temple the evangelist Luke notes: "And when they had performed everything according to the law of the Lord, *they returned to Galilee*, to their own city, Nazareth. And the child grew and became strong, filled with wisdom; and the favor of God was upon him" (Lk 2:39–40).

But *according to Matthew's text*, a very important event took place before the return to Galilee, an event in which divine providence once again had recourse to Joseph. We read: "Now when [the magi] had departed, behold, an angel of the Lord appeared to Joseph in a dream and said, *'Rise, take the child and his mother, and flee to Egypt*, and remain there till I tell you; for Herod is about to search for the child, to destroy him'" (Mt 2:13). Herod learned from the magi who came from the East about the birth of the "king of the Jews" (Mt 2:2). And when the magi departed, he "sent and killed all the male children in Bethlehem and in all that region who were two years old or under" (Mt 2:16). By killing them all, he wished to kill the newborn "king of the Jews" whom he had heard about. And so, Joseph, having been warned in a dream, "took the child and his mother by night, and *departed to Egypt*, and remained there *until the death of Herod.* This was to fulfill what the Lord had spoken by the prophet, 'Out of Egypt I have called my son'" (Mt 2:14–15; cf. Hos 11:1).

And so Jesus's way back to Nazareth from Bethlehem passed through Egypt. Just as Israel had followed the path of the exodus "from the condition of slavery" in order to begin the Old Covenant, *so Joseph, guardian and cooperator in the providential mystery of God*, even in exile watched over the one who brings about the New Covenant.

Jesus's Stay in the Temple

15. From the time of the annunciation, both Joseph and Mary found themselves, in a certain sense, *at the heart of the mystery* hidden for ages in the mind of God, a mystery which had taken on flesh: *"The Word became flesh and dwelt among us"* (Jn 1:14). He dwelt among men, within the surroundings of *the Holy Family of Nazareth*—one of many families in this small town in Galilee, one of the many families of the land of Israel. There Jesus "grew and became strong, filled with wisdom; and the favor of God was upon him" (Lk 2:40). The Gospels summarize in a few words the *long period of the "hidden" life*, during which Jesus prepared himself for his messianic mission. Only one episode from this "hidden time" is described in *the Gospel of Luke: the Passover in Jerusalem when Jesus was twelve years old.* Together with Mary and Joseph, Jesus took part in the feast as a young pilgrim. "And when the feast was ended, as they were returning, the boy Jesus stayed behind in Jerusalem. His parents did not know it" (Lk 2:43). After a day's journey, they noticed his absence and began to search "among their kinsfolk and acquaintances" (Lk 2:44). "After three days *they found him in the temple*, sitting among the teachers, listening to them and asking them questions; and all who heard him were amazed at

his understanding and his answers" (Lk 2:46–47). Mary asked: "Son, why have you treated us so? *Behold, your father and I have been looking for you anxiously*" (Lk 2:48). The answer Jesus gave was such that "they did not understand the saying which he spoke to them." He had said, "How is it that you sought me? Did you not know *that I must be in my Father's house?*" (Lk 2:49–50)

Joseph, of whom Mary had just used the words "your father," heard this answer. That, after all, is what all the people said and thought: Jesus was the son (as was supposed) of Joseph" (Lk 3:23). Nonetheless, the reply of Jesus in the Temple brought once again to the mind of his "presumed father" what he had heard on that night twelve years earlier: "Joseph . . . do not fear to take Mary your wife, for *that which is conceived in her is of the Holy Spirit.*" From that time onward he knew that he was a guardian of the mystery of God, and it was *precisely this mystery* that the twelve-year-old *Jesus brought to mind*: "I must be in my Father's house."

The Support and Education of Jesus of Nazareth

16. The growth of Jesus "in wisdom and in stature, and in favor with God and man" (Lk 2:52) took place within the Holy Family under the eyes of Joseph, who had the important task of "raising" Jesus, that is, feeding, clothing, and educating him in the Law and in a trade, in keeping with the duties of a father.

In the Eucharistic Sacrifice, the Church venerates the memory of Mary the ever Virgin Mother of God and the memory of Saint Joseph,[29] because "he fed him whom the faithful must eat as the bread of eternal life."[30]

For his part, Jesus "was obedient to them" (Lk 2:51), respectfully returning the affection of his "parents." In this way he wished to sanctify the obligations of the family and of work, which he performed at the side of Joseph.

PONDER

Often we think of faith and religion as an experience that sets us free or elevates us. While such experiences are important, they are the fruit of a much deeper reality. God calls us to freedom *through* obedience. There is no other way. John Paul II begins his meditation on the guardianship of Saint Joseph by referring to the teaching of Vatican II, which states that when God reveals himself we are called to make "the full submission of intellect and will" to him (*RC* 4). Mary did this by speaking her *fiat* (see Lk 1:38), while Joseph did it through his actions (*RC* 4). Each was obedient to the role they had to play in the plan of salvation, and so they became the "first guardians" of the divine mystery.

The incarnation and the passion of Jesus are indissolubly and organically united. Thus, Joseph was intimately united to the *passion* of Jesus through his role in the *incarnation* and childhood of Christ. He was the first to share in the faith of Mary concerning the birth and nature of Jesus (*RC* 5), and he was the divinely appointed father-protector of the child. To recognize his intimate involvement in the salvific plan, John XXIII had Saint Joseph's name inserted into the Roman Canon of the Mass (Eucharistic Prayer I) (*RC* 6). This was further underscored on May 1, 2013, when Pope Francis issued the decree *Paternas Vice* (*Fatherly Care*) and added Saint Joseph's name to Eucharistic Prayers II, III, and IV.

For John Paul II, it is critical to confirm the realism of both the family and the marriage of Joseph and Mary. If they are not real, then they cannot stand as a pattern for others. The question, of course, is how can a celibate marriage truly be a "real" marriage? John Paul II answers this by looking at what constitutes a marriage. Making a total gift of oneself to the other in freedom is at the heart of it. Conjugal relations are the privileged expression of this. But these relations *express* a deeper reality: the spousal gift of self. Even in conjugal relations one can selfishly use another and withhold the gift of self. In contrast, as Saint Augustine and Saint Thomas teach, the relationship of Mary and Joseph had the reality of "an indivisible union" of souls and hearts, made in complete freedom and with proper consent (*RC* 7). So even though there were no conjugal relations, all of Augustine's essential elements of a marriage were present: offspring (Jesus), fidelity (there was no adultery), and the sacrament (there was no divorce) (*RC* 7). We need to remember that marriage comes into being through the consent of the couple (see *CCC,* no. 1626) who thus are truly married even before they have conjugal relations. Hence, we see that the purposes of marriage were preeminently fulfilled in Joseph and Mary.

But is the Holy Family "real"? Is Joseph a "real" father or merely an outsider? John Paul II states that Joseph's fatherhood was clearly given a juridical basis through his marriage to Mary. (In Matthew, the lineage of Jesus is legally traced through Joseph's line.) The pope further notes that Joseph possesses both fatherly authority over Jesus and love for the child, and that both come from the heavenly Father (*RC* 8).

Joseph serves Jesus directly by being his father. As head of the family, Joseph makes "a total gift of self" (*RC* 8), serving by yielding up his life through his actions in service to his family. In this manner, Joseph lives out the true meaning of paternal authority and headship as understood in Scripture. Joseph's aim is to bring his family into fullness of being. The holy couple is therefore archetypical and shows us the nature and mission of the family (*RC* 7). It is to be a place founded on the gift of love, where relationships share in God's redeeming love for humanity (*RC* 7). The family thus reflects the Church and becomes, in fact, the Church in miniature.

This takes concrete form particularly in Saint Joseph's ministry to his family. John Paul II reviews the various events in the early life of Jesus to show the essential role Joseph played. He discerned God's will (the flight to Egypt); he proclaimed the mission of Jesus (the naming); he acted as a foil to the divine fatherhood (the finding in the Temple), etc. (*RC* 9–16).

Thus Joseph, both in his marriage and his role as father, becomes an exemplar of how one cooperates with God in his salvific plan. Joseph shows us how to walk in obedience and discern God's will in the day-to-day decisions that arise in our families and lives.

1. Joseph was not only a just man, but also an obedient one. Salvation history depended upon his obedience to God's call to protect the fragile life of the divine child. Do I see obedience as a major part of my Christian walk? Why is obedience so important? To

what and to whom are we obedient: to our thoughts, our ideas, our feelings? What role does the Church's teaching magisterium play in our call to obedience?

2. It is sometimes difficult to understand how being one in the spirit (or mind) but "not in the flesh" (*RC* 7) is really an expression of marital love. Can a marriage exist, however, if it is based only on physical reactions and activities without a deep spiritual communion? If conjugal relations are the expression of the couple's spiritual communion, how can a spouse deepen and strengthen that communion?

3. Joseph served by doing; he said yes to God through his actions. Do you sometimes talk but not follow through with actions? Can you think of a specific instance when this may have occurred? In the future how can you avoid not following through?

Pray

Jesus, you taught that we will know people "by their fruits" (Mt 7:20). Joseph was a man of action, not of words. No word of Joseph's is recorded, but we do have the record of his many faithful deeds by which he protected you and brought you up in the faith. Grant that our lives will be marked by fewer words and more obedient actions. Give us an obedient heart, that we may please you and become more like your foster father, Saint Joseph. Amen.

Act

Identify two or three areas in your life where you habitually fail to follow through on your promises or obligations. Devise a realistic plan by which you will choose to be obedient to God's will in order to carry out your commitments.

PART III

A Just Man—A Husband

17. In the course of that pilgrimage of faith which was his life, Joseph, like Mary, remained faithful to God's call until the end. While Mary's life was the bringing to fullness of that *fiat* first spoken at the annunciation, *at the moment of Joseph's own "annunciation"* he said nothing; instead he simply "*did* as the angel of the Lord commanded him" (Mt 1:24). And *this first "doing" became the beginning of "Joseph's way."* The Gospels do not record any word ever spoken by Joseph along that way. But *the silence of Joseph* has its own special eloquence, for thanks to that silence we can understand the truth of the Gospel's judgment that he was "a just man" (Mt 1:19).

One must come to understand this truth, for it contains *one of the most important testimonies concerning man and his vocation.* Through many generations the Church has read this testimony with ever greater attention and with deeper understanding, drawing, as it were, "what is new and what is old" (Mt 13:52) from the storehouse of the noble figure of Joseph.

18. Above all, the "just" man of Nazareth possesses the clear characteristics of a husband. Luke refers to Mary as "a virgin betrothed to a man whose name was Joseph" (Lk 1:27). Even before the "mystery hidden for ages" (Eph 3:9) began to be fulfilled, the Gospels set before us *the image of husband and wife.* According to Jewish custom, marriage took place in two stages: first, the legal, or true marriage was celebrated, and then, only after a certain period of time, the husband brought the wife into his own house. Thus, before he lived with Mary, Joseph was already her "husband." *Mary, however, preserved her deep desire to give herself exclusively to God.* One may well ask how this desire of Mary's could be reconciled with a "wedding." The answer can only come from the saving events as they unfold, from the special action of God himself. From the moment of the annunciation, Mary knew that *she was to fulfill her virginal desire* to give herself exclusively and fully to God precisely *by becoming the Mother of God's Son.* Becoming a Mother by the power of the Holy Spirit was the form taken by her gift of self: a form which God himself expected of the Virgin Mary, who was "betrothed" to Joseph. Mary uttered her *fiat.* The fact that Mary was "betrothed" to Joseph was *part of the very plan of God.* This is pointed out by Luke and especially by Matthew. The words spoken to Joseph are very significant: "Do not fear to take Mary *your wife,* for that which has been conceived in her is of the Holy Spirit" (Mt 1:20). These words explain the mystery of Joseph's wife: In her motherhood Mary is a virgin. In her, "the Son of the Most High" assumed a human body and became "the Son of Man."

Addressing Joseph through the words of the angel, God speaks to him *as the husband of the Virgin of Nazareth.* What took place in her through the power of the Holy Spirit also *confirmed in a special way the marriage bond* which already existed between Joseph and Mary. God's messenger was clear in what he said to Joseph: "Do not fear to take Mary *your wife* into your home." Hence, what had taken place earlier, namely, Joseph's marriage to Mary, happened in accord with God's will and was meant to endure. In her divine motherhood Mary had to continue to live as "a virgin, the wife of her husband" (cf. Lk 1:27).

19. In the words of the "annunciation" by night, Joseph not only heard the divine truth concerning his wife's indescribable vocation; he *also heard once again the truth about his own vocation.* This "just" man, who, in the spirit of the noblest traditions of the Chosen People, loved the Virgin of Nazareth and was bound to her by a husband's love, was once again called by God to this love.

"Joseph did as the angel of the Lord commanded him; he took his wife" into his home (Mt 1:24); what was conceived in Mary was "of the Holy Spirit." From expressions such as these are we not to suppose that his *love as a man was also given new birth by the Holy Spirit*? Are we not to think that the love of God which has been poured forth into the human heart through the Holy Spirit (cf. Rom 5:5) molds every human love to perfection? This love of God also molds—in a completely unique way—the love of husband and wife, deepening within it everything of human worth and beauty, everything that bespeaks an exclusive gift of self, a covenant between persons, and an authentic communion according to the model of the Blessed Trinity.

"Joseph . . . took his wife; *but he knew her not*, until she had borne a son" (Mt 1:24–25). These words indicate *another kind of closeness in marriage.* The deep spiritual closeness arising from marital union and the interpersonal contact between man and woman have their definitive origin in the Spirit, the Giver of Life (cf. Jn 6:63). *Joseph, in obedience to the Spirit, found in the Spirit the source of love*, the conjugal love which he experienced as a man. And this love proved to be greater than this "just man" could ever have expected within the limits of his human heart.

20. In the liturgy, Mary is celebrated as "united to Joseph, the just man, by a bond of marital and virginal love."[31] There are really two kinds of love here, both of which *together* represent the mystery of the Church—virgin and spouse—as symbolized in the marriage of Mary and Joseph. "Virginity or celibacy for the sake of the kingdom of God not only does not contradict the dignity of marriage but presupposes and confirms it. Marriage and virginity are two ways of expressing and living the one mystery of the covenant of God with his people,"[32] the covenant which is a communion of love between God and human beings.

Through his complete self-sacrifice, Joseph expressed his generous love for the Mother of God, and gave her a husband's "gift of self." Even though he decided to draw back so as not to interfere in the plan of God which was coming to pass in Mary, Joseph obeyed the explicit command of the angel and look Mary into his home, while respecting the fact that she belonged exclusively to God.

On the other hand, it was from his marriage to Mary that Joseph derived his singular dignity and his rights in regard to Jesus. "It is certain that the dignity of the Mother of God is so exalted that nothing could be more sublime; yet because Mary was united to Joseph by the bond of marriage, there can be no doubt but that *Joseph approached as no other person ever could* that eminent dignity whereby the Mother of God towers above all creatures. Since marriage is the highest degree of association and friendship involving by its very nature a communion of goods, it follows that God, by giving Joseph to the Virgin, did not give him to her only as a companion for life, a witness of her virginity and protector of her honor; he also gave Joseph to Mary in order that *he might share*, through the marriage pact, in her own sublime greatness."[33]

21. This *bond of charity was the core of the Holy Family's life*, first in the poverty of Bethlehem, then in their exile in Egypt, and later in the house of Nazareth. The Church deeply venerates this family, and proposes it as the model of all families. Inserted directly in the mystery of the Incarnation, the family of Nazareth has its own special mystery. And in this mystery, as in the Incarnation, one finds a true fatherhood: *the human form of the family of the Son of God*, a true human family, formed by the divine mystery. *In this family, Joseph is the father: his fatherhood* is not one that derives from begetting offspring; but neither is it an "apparent" or merely

"substitute" fatherhood. Rather, it is one that *fully shares in authentic human fatherhood* and the mission of a father in the family. This is a consequence of the hypostatic union: humanity taken up into the unity of the Divine Person of the Word-Son, Jesus Christ. Together with human nature, *all that is human, and especially the family*—as the first dimension of man's existence in the world—*is also taken up* in Christ. Within this context, Joseph's human fatherhood was also "taken up" in the mystery of Christ's Incarnation.

On the basis of this principle, the words which Mary spoke to the twelve-year-old Jesus in the Temple take on their full significance: *"Your father and I . . .* have been looking for you." This is no conventional phrase: Mary's words to Jesus show the complete reality of the Incarnation present in the mystery of the family of Nazareth. From the beginning, *Joseph accepted with the "obedience of faith"* his human fatherhood over Jesus. And thus, following the light of the Holy Spirit who gives himself to human beings through faith, he certainly came to discover ever more fully *the indescribable gift that was his human fatherhood.*

Ponder

Today we speak of the "little way" of Saint Thérèse of Lisieux, a way to grow in the spiritual life by following her emphasis on simplicity. Similarly, John Paul II speaks of "Joseph's way" (*RC* 17). What this means is not readily apparent, but the Holy Father shows that this "way" is intimately tied to "the silence of Joseph" (*RC* 17). It is striking that there are no recorded words of Saint Joseph. His silence underlines the fact that Joseph reveals his character and his faith not in *words* but in *actions*.

Scripture reveals Joseph to be a "just" man. In the state of *original justice* in Eden, man had perfect communion with God and thus had perfect control over his own body *to serve the other*. Lust did not exist, only the genuine gift of self did. Redemption is already active within the marriage of Joseph and Mary; as such we can begin to see the true nature of human marriage, although theirs contains so many paradoxes.

The Scriptures link the Incarnation to Joseph's being the husband of Mary. Before the Incarnation occurred, we have set before us "the image of husband and wife" in Mary and Joseph (*RC* 18). This conjugal context is *the space* in which the Incarnation took place. Jews had a two-stage marriage process (*RC* 18). In the first stage, one became a *legal* spouse. Only at a later stage did the man take (in Hebrew, *laqak*) the wife and consummate the marriage. In Joseph's case, unbeknownst to him, the mystery of the Incarnation intervened between the two stages, setting up a seeming contradiction.

As John Paul II notes, Mary had desired to give herself exclusively to God (*RC* 18). In the annunciation this longing was fulfilled. Mary gives herself to God and she conceives. This shows forth what is at the heart of all human marriage: the desire to give oneself exclusively to another. But how can such exclusivity to God be safeguarded if she then enters into the fullness of marriage with Joseph? With men this is impossible . . . but not with God. He intervenes directly, sending an angel to Joseph who says, "Do not be afraid to take Mary your wife into your home" (Mt 1:20; *RC* 18). Mary would remain a virgin and yet be wife and mother; Joseph would be a true husband and father, yet without conjugal relations. In this way the two types of mutually exclusive loves, the virginal and the spousal, were united in this holy couple (*RC* 20).

Joseph's own "annunciation" by the angel reveals to him "the truth about his own vocation" (*RC* 19). God calls him back to the spousal love he had for Mary. He is not to be afraid. In obeying, a new vista of God's work is opened. Joseph's own love as a man, *as a husband*, is given new birth, new meaning through the Holy Spirit (*RC* 19). Through obedience, Joseph discovers in the Spirit "the source of love," a love he could not have imagined. The inner logic of marital love is revealed.

Precisely because he makes a complete gift of self to Mary (i.e., sacrifices himself for her), Joseph desires to preserve what is at the core of Mary's vocation: her exclusive belonging to God (*RC* 20). In this case, the lack of fleshly consummation does not impede or block their union; rather it becomes the expression of a love transformed in the Spirit (*RC* 19).

1. We often cling to our old habits, our familiar ways of doing things. Saint Joseph was called to live out his life in a totally new way. The rights and privileges of marital life were to yield to a different and fuller union. He had to allow God to transform his understanding of human love. Do I struggle when God seems to be calling me to something new? Do I easily yield to promptings of the Spirit, especially if I must enter into uncharted water? What can I do to make myself more open to God's will in my life?

2. By making a complete gift of self to Mary, Joseph thought of her rather than himself. In walking in obedience to God's word to him, he discovered his own human love for Mary was transformed. Do I truly put others ahead of myself? Do I understand what making the gift of self to my spouse or to another person is all about? How can I identify those areas in my marriage or in my relationships with others where I am self-centered rather than other-centered? How can I bring change into my life so that I begin learning to serve those around me?

Pray

Father, you have given us Saint Joseph as an example of a husband who gave himself unreservedly to his wife and child. Knowing himself, he gave that self to those he loved and thereby created a holy family. As you spoke to Joseph through an angel, speak to us so we can hear and obey you. Speak to us about those areas where we need to let go of fear so we can begin to love. Speak to us about where we must go so that we can become whole and holy. We ask this in your Son's name. Amen.

Act

Identify a place in your marriage or family life where you habitually act selfishly. Bring this to confession. Think of one concrete way you could begin to put the other's needs ahead of your own.

PART IV

Work As an Expression of Love

22. *Work was the daily expression of love in the life of the family of Nazareth.* The Gospel specifies the kind of work Joseph did in order to support his family: he was a carpenter. This simple word sums up Joseph's entire life. For Jesus, these were hidden years, the years to which Luke refers after recounting the episode that occurred in the Temple: "And he went down with them and came to Nazareth, and was obedient to them" (Lk 2:51). This *"submission"* or obedience of Jesus in the house of Nazareth should be *understood as a sharing in the work of Joseph.* Having learned the work of his presumed father, he was known as "the carpenter's son." If the family of Nazareth is an example and model for human families, in the order of salvation and holiness, so, too, by analogy, is Jesus's work at the side of Joseph the carpenter. In our own day, the Church has emphasized this by instituting the liturgical memorial of Saint Joseph the Worker on May 1. *Human work,* and especially manual labor, *receive special prominence in the Gospel.* Along with the

humanity of the Son of God, work too has been taken up in the mystery of the Incarnation, and *has also been redeemed in a special way*. At the workbench where he plied his trade together with Jesus, Joseph brought human work closer to the mystery of the redemption.

23. In the human growth of Jesus "in wisdom, age, and grace," the *virtue of industriousness* played a notable role, since "work is a human good" which "transforms nature" and makes man "in a sense, more human."[34]

The importance of work in human life demands that its meaning be known and assimilated in order to "help all people to come closer to God, the Creator and Redeemer, to participate in his salvific plan for man and the world, and to deepen . . . friendship with Christ in their lives, by accepting, through faith, a living participation in his threefold mission as Priest, Prophet, and King."[35]

24. What is crucially important here is the sanctification of daily life, a sanctification which each person must acquire according to his or her own state, and one which can be promoted according to a model accessible to all people: "Saint Joseph is the model of those humble ones that Christianity raises up to great destinies; . . . he is the proof that in order to be a good and genuine follower of Christ, there is no need of great things—it is enough to have the common, simple, and human virtues, but they need to be true and authentic."[36]

Ponder

Often we see human work as something exterior to the person, the unsavory price we have to pay for existence. We may try to avoid it, or at least reduce it to its bare minimum so we can get on with our *real* life. But in the Holy Family work takes on a totally different value. It is intimately tied to love and is, in fact, an expression of it. There is no dualism here. There is an organic unity between who Mary, Joseph, and Jesus were and the work they carried out together. Work becomes for them a "way" of sanctification.

Joseph is designated as a "carpenter." This simple word, as John Paul II notes, "sums up Joseph's entire life" (*RC* 22). It is who he was. In being a just man, all aspects of Joseph's life were guided by the Holy Spirit, including his work. Because he lived within the center of the Incarnation, his work was also assumed into the center of this salvific event. As John Paul II further notes, when Jesus returned from the Temple in Jerusalem and "was obedient to them," it meant that he had "a sharing in the work of Joseph" (*RC* 22). In assuming our humanity, Christ redeemed all of its aspects, including work and our relationship to it (*RC* 22).

As a Jewish father who had the responsibility to teach his son a trade, Joseph would have brought Jesus into his place of work, the carpentry shop. In fact, Jesus became known as "the carpenter's son" (Mt 13:55). By training Jesus to be skilled in his craft and to take pride in what he made, Joseph was bringing *all* human work "closer to the mystery of the redemption" (*RC* 22). And if the Son of God worked, then work must have a profound value and meaning in the life of each person. Through his own engagement with labor, Jesus redeemed man's relationship to it.

In the encyclical *Laborem Exercens*, John Paul II examined the role of work and observed that the virtue of industriousness played a key role in Jesus's growth (as it does in every human life). Work is a dynamic force that can transform us and, in a certain sense, make us more fully human (*RC* 23). We have only to remember that Adam was commanded by God to work in the Garden. The paradisal form of life *included* work.

The problem, only hinted at by John Paul II, is that in our fallen state the meaning of work has become clouded and disordered. How then do we regain a right relationship with work? Joseph gives us the example. We need to invite Jesus into our work and understand it as a way of coming "closer to God" (*RC* 23). Jesus brings his nature as prophet, priest, and king to his labor, thereby sanctifying it. Similarly, we who have Christ living in us (see Gal 2:20) need to bring Christ into all our activities. The key is to learn to allow God's holiness to enter into all aspects of our daily life, including our work. In this way, human labor becomes sacramental, an expression of Christ living in us.

1. John Paul II writes that work was the expression of love in the Holy Family. We need to allow Jesus to

redeem and heal how we think about work. How do I look upon work in my life? As drudgery? As something I must put up with? Am I able to see work as a way of living out my faith?

2. In *Laborem Exercens* John Paul II tells us that work transforms not only nature but, in a certain sense, it also transforms us (*LE* 40). The question here is not the type of work we do, but how we understand its purpose. We need to see our work, whatever it may be, as a way of serving God and others. Can I recognize how I serve others through my work? What should be my attitude toward my employers, my coworkers, and/or the people whom my business serves?

3. In 1955 Pius XII established the Feast of Saint Joseph the Worker, thereby commemorating human work in the Church's liturgy and proposing Saint Joseph as a model for all Christians. Do I consider my own work as something worthy of being commemorated at Mass? How can my work be related to the sacrifice of the Mass and to Jesus's work of redemption?

PRAY

Saint Joseph, as a man you worked in your carpentry shop. Your hands grew rough and sinewy after many years of toil. In the midst of your labor you took Jesus and showed him how to become a man of work, a man dedicated to the job that was set before him. Joseph, pray for us, that we may come to know the meaning and purpose of work in our lives and see how in all we do we are serving God. Amen.

Act

Before you begin your next day at work, or whatever project you are involved in, pause a moment and ask God to open your eyes so that you can perceive how you are serving him and others through this work.

PART V

The Primacy of the Interior Life

25. The same aura of silence that envelops everything else about Joseph also shrouds his work as a carpenter in the house of Nazareth. It is, however, *a silence that reveals in a special way the inner portrait of the man.* The Gospels speak exclusively of what Joseph "did." Still, they allow us to discover in his "actions"—shrouded in silence as they are—an aura of *deep contemplation.* Joseph was in daily contact with the mystery "hidden from ages past," and which "dwelt" under his roof. This explains, for example, why Saint Teresa of Jesus, the great reformer of the Carmelites, promoted the renewal of veneration to Saint Joseph in Western Christianity.

26. The total sacrifice, whereby Joseph surrendered his whole existence to the demands of the Messiah's coming into his home, becomes understandable only in the light of his profound interior life. It was from this interior life that "very singular commands and consolations came, bringing him also the logic and strength that belong to simple and clear souls, and giving him the power of making great

decisions—such as the decision to put his liberty immediately at the disposition of the divine designs, to make over to them also his legitimate human calling, his conjugal happiness, to accept the conditions, the responsibility, and the burden of a family, but, through an incomparable virginal love, to renounce that natural conjugal love that is the foundation and nourishment of the family."[37]

This submission to God, this readiness of will to dedicate oneself to all that serves him, is really nothing less than that *exercise of devotion* which constitutes one expression of the virtue of religion.[38]

27. The communion of life between Joseph and Jesus leads us to consider once again the mystery of the Incarnation, precisely in reference to the humanity of Jesus as the efficacious instrument of his divinity for the purpose of sanctifying man: "By virtue of his divinity, Christ's human actions were salvific for us, causing grace within us, either by merit or by a certain efficacy."[39]

Among those actions, the Gospel writers highlight those which have to do with the Paschal Mystery, but they also underscore the importance of physical contact with Jesus for healing (cf., for example, Mk 1:41), and the influence Jesus exercised upon John the Baptist when they were both in their mothers' wombs (cf. Lk 1:41–44).

As we have seen, the apostolic witness did not neglect the story of Jesus's birth, his circumcision, his presentation in the Temple, his flight into Egypt, and his hidden life in Nazareth. It recognized the "mystery" of grace present in each of these saving "acts," inasmuch as they all share the same source of love: the divinity of Christ. If through Christ's humanity this love shone on all mankind, the first beneficiaries were undoubtedly those whom the divine will had most intimately associated with itself: Mary, the Mother of Jesus, and Joseph, his presumed father.[40]

Why should the "fatherly" love of Joseph not have had an influence upon the "filial" love of Jesus? And, vice versa, why should the "filial" love of Jesus not have had an influence upon the "fatherly" love of Joseph, thus leading to a further deepening of their unique relationship? Those souls most sensitive to the impulses of divine love have rightly seen in Joseph a brilliant example of the interior life.

Furthermore, in Joseph the apparent tension between the active and the contemplative life finds an ideal harmony that is only possible for those who possess the perfection of charity. Following Saint Augustine's well-known distinction between the love of the truth (*caritas veritatis*) and the practical demands of love (*necessitas caritatis*),[41] we can say that Joseph experienced both *love of the truth*—that pure contemplative love of the divine Truth which radiated from the humanity of Christ—and *the demands of love*: that equally pure and selfless love required for his vocation to safeguard and develop the humanity of Jesus, which was inseparably linked to his divinity.

Ponder

A perennial problem in the Church has been the question of whether the contemplative life or the life of action is more important. Is true Christian religion best seen in those agitating for justice in our society or in those dedicating themselves to a life of prayer? In "Primacy of the Interior Life" John Paul II shows us that this is only an "apparent tension" (*RC* 27).

In the person who is perfected in charity (i.e., the saint), this tension is dissolved because *action* and *contemplation* are both present and have the right relation to each other. It is not a question of *either–or* but of *both-and* in a proper relationship. John Paul II proposes Saint Joseph as a preeminent example of how to live this out. In some ways it is odd to think of Joseph as a contemplative, because he was primarily a man of action. Yet all his actions, his total gift of self to Mary and Jesus, sprang from the depth of his interior life. There can be no truly human action without an authentic interior life.

Now think of Joseph. Every day he was with Jesus, worked and played with him. Uniquely, all of Joseph's life and actions were lived within the presence of Jesus. Daily his gaze would be upon his reputed son. Thus his daily life was an act of contemplation (*RC* 26).

To understand this better, we need only think about the effect Jesus had on those who were open to God. Many were healed simply through physical contact with Christ. When the baby John in Elizabeth's womb sensed the presence of Christ in Mary, he leapt for joy (see Lk 1:41). Why? Because Christ is always mediating grace. Therefore all his actions become filled with grace. As John Paul II observes, the Scriptures record the physical events in Christ's life (his birth, circumcision, the flight into Egypt) to show that divine grace was present in them. It is through the humanity of Christ that we experience his divinity (*RC* 27). This is especially true when we encounter Jesus in his Body and Blood in the Eucharist. Joseph lived daily with Christ's divine humanity.

Saint Joseph's interior life can also be observed through the effect it had on how he carried out his vocation. How could an ordinary man live a life that required heroic virtue? He was to carry out the full responsibilities of a husband while renouncing the "natural conjugal love that is the foundation and nourishment" of marriage (*RC* 26). He was to take on the awe-inducing responsibility of being father to the Son of God in a fallen world that violently raged against this holy child. Only a profound interior life, a life centered on Jesus (for that is what contemplation is) could allow one to so act. This profound and integrated point of daily contemplation of Jesus provided the logic of Joseph's actions. It also provided the strength for him to continually say yes to his daunting vocation (*RC* 25). Joseph thus became a man of action precisely because he was a man of contemplation.

1. The very fact that no word of Saint Joseph was ever recorded can be seen to accentuate his deep and rich interior life. Rather than use external words, Joseph experienced a deep interior communion with God that issued forth in faith-filled actions. Do I use words to protect myself from others and from God? Am I afraid to be quiet with God, afraid he might guide me in a direction I am not comfortable with?

2. Joseph, because he was the foster father of Jesus, had regular, daily contact with him. His was a unique situation where he could experience the divine presence at almost any moment of the day. Do I recognize the Eucharist as a bodily encounter with Jesus? What are the ways in which I can try to come into contact with Jesus each day? Am I making a serous effort in this regard?

Pray

Lord, we love you but seem to have so little time to pursue you. We are so busy, so rushed. Give us wisdom and discernment, that we may order our days aright. May our goal always be to seek an ever-deeper communion with you. Help us to live so that our actions proceed only from our communion with you. Amen.

Act

Each day for the next week, set aside fifteen minutes in which you do something concretely to deepen your communion with God. Do whatever might draw you into greater communion with God: read Scripture, go to Eucharistic adoration, spend some time in quiet prayer, etc.

Part VI

Patron of the Church in Our Day

28. At a difficult time in the Church's history, Pope Pius IX, wishing to place her under the powerful patronage of the holy patriarch Joseph, declared him "Patron of the Catholic Church."[42] For Pius IX this was no idle gesture, since by virtue of the sublime dignity which God has granted to his most faithful servant Joseph, "the Church, after the Blessed Virgin, his spouse, has always held him in great honor and showered him with praise, having recourse to him amid tribulations."[43]

What are the reasons for such great confidence? Leo XIII explained it in this way: "The reasons why Saint Joseph must be considered the special patron of the Church, and the Church in turn draws exceeding hope from his care and patronage, chiefly arise from his having been the husband of Mary and the presumed father of Jesus . . . , Joseph was in his day the lawful and natural guardian, head, and defender of the Holy Family. . . . It is thus fitting and most worthy of Joseph's dignity that, in the same way that he once kept unceasing holy watch over the family of Nazareth, so now does he protect and defend with his heavenly patronage the Church of Christ."[44]

29. This patronage must be invoked as ever necessary for the Church, not only as a defense against all dangers, but also, and indeed primarily, as an impetus for her renewed commitment to evangelization in the world and to re-evangelization in those lands and nations where—as I wrote in the Apostolic Exhortation *Christifideles Laici*—"religion and the Christian life were formerly flourishing and . . . are now put to a hard test."[45] In order to bring the first proclamation of Christ, or to bring it anew wherever it has been neglected or forgotten, the Church has need of special "power from on high" (cf. Lk 24:49; Acts 1:8): a gift of the Spirit of the Lord, a gift which is not unrelated to the intercession and example of his saints.

30. Besides trusting in Joseph's sure protection, the Church also trusts in his noble example, which transcends all individual states of life and serves as a model for the entire Christian community, whatever the condition and duties of each of its members may be.

As the *Constitution on Divine Revelation* of the Second Vatican Council has said, the basic attitude of the entire Church must be that of "hearing the word of God with reverence,"[46] an absolute readiness to serve faithfully God's salvific will revealed in Jesus. Already at the beginning of human redemption, after Mary, we find the model of obedience made incarnate in Saint Joseph, the man known for having faithfully carried out God's commands.

Pope Paul VI invited us to invoke Joseph's patronage "as the Church has been wont to do in these recent times, for herself in the first place, with a spontaneous theological reflection on the marriage of divine and human action in the great economy of the Redemption, in which economy the first—the divine one—is wholly sufficient unto itself, while the second—the human action which is ours—though capable of nothing (cf. Jn 15:5), is never dispensed from a humble but conditional and ennobling collaboration. The Church also calls upon Joseph as her protector because of a profound and ever-present desire to reinvigorate her ancient life with true evangelical virtues, such as shine forth in Saint Joseph."[47]

31. The Church transforms these needs into prayer. Recalling that God wished to entrust the beginnings of our redemption to the faithful care of Saint Joseph, she asks God to grant that she may faithfully cooperate in the work of salvation; that she may receive the same faithfulness and purity of heart that inspired Joseph in serving the Incarnate Word; and that she may walk before God in the ways of holiness and justice, following Joseph's example and through his intercession.[48]

One hundred years ago, Pope Leo XIII had already exhorted the Catholic world to pray for the protection of Saint Joseph, Patron of the whole Church. The Encyclical Epistle *Quamquam Pluries* appealed to Joseph's "fatherly love . . . for the child Jesus" and commended to him, as "the provident guardian of the divine Family," "the beloved inheritance which Jesus Christ purchased by his blood." Since that time—as I recalled at the beginning of this Exhortation

—*the Church has implored the protection of Saint Joseph* on the basis of "that sacred bond of charity which united him to the Immaculate Virgin Mother of God," and the Church has commended to Joseph all of her cares, including those dangers which threaten the human family.

Even *today* we have *many reasons to pray in a similar way*: "Most beloved father, dispel the evil of falsehood and sin . . . graciously assist us from heaven in our struggle with the powers of darkness . . . and just as once you saved the child Jesus from mortal danger, so now defend God's holy Church from the snares of her enemies and from all adversity."[49] Today we still have *good reason to commend everyone to Saint Joseph*.

32. It is my heartfelt wish that these reflections on the person of Saint Joseph will renew in us the prayerful devotion which my Predecessor called for a century ago. Our prayers and *the very person of Joseph have renewed significance for the Church in our day* in light of the third Christian millennium.

The *Second Vatican Council made all of us sensitive once again* to the "great things which God has done," and to that *"economy of salvation"* of which Saint Joseph was a special minister. Commending ourselves, then, to the protection of him to whose custody God "entrusted his greatest and most precious treasures,"[50] *let us at the same time learn from him how to be servants of the "economy of salvation."* May Saint Joseph become for all of us an exceptional teacher in the service of *Christ's saving mission*, a mission which is the responsibility of each and every member of the Church:

husbands and wives, parents, those who live by the work of their hands or by any other kind of work, those called to the contemplative life, and those called to the apostolate.

This just man, who bore within himself the entire heritage of the Old Covenant, was also *brought into the "beginning" of the New and Eternal Covenant in Jesus Christ*. May he show us the paths of this saving Covenant as we stand at the threshold of the next millennium, in which there must be a continuation and further development of the "fullness of time" that belongs to the ineffable mystery of the Incarnation of the Word.

May Saint Joseph obtain for the Church and for the world, as well as for each of us, the blessing of the Father, Son, and Holy Spirit.

Given at Rome, in Saint Peter's, on August 15—the Solemnity of the Assumption of the Blessed Virgin Mary—in the year 1989, the eleventh of my Pontificate.

Joannes Paulus PP. II

PONDER

It is easy to fall into two opposing errors concerning salvation. One is to think it depends only on human effort. The other is to think that God does everything and we do nothing. Neither position takes the Incarnation seriously but sees the human person in dualistic terms. Instead, John Paul II shows how both divine and human actions work together in the process of salvation, echoing Saint Paul's teaching in his Letter to the Philippians 2:12–13. Three intersecting truths help explain this.

First, God's action in saving us is "wholly sufficient unto itself" (*RC* 30). Being all-powerful, God does not require help from us. He is the *source* of salvation. Hence, everything is based on grace.

Second, our human actions—*on their own*—are "capable of nothing" (*RC* 30). That is, whenever we separate ourselves from God, our human actions are empty, incapable of achieving salvation. Here John Paul II refers to John 15, where Jesus teaches that we are the branches while he is the main vine. To be fruitful, we have to abide in him. *Human activity, by itself, cannot produce fruit.*

Third, God always respects the human freedom and dignity he created. Therefore, while not needing to do so, he *always* invites each person to participate with him. He calls us to "a humble but conditional . . . collaboration" in this mighty work (*RC* 30). We do not save ourselves. Nonetheless, God never dispenses us from *cooperating* with him in this great mystery (*RC* 30).

Through his obedience, Joseph became a preeminent model of cooperation. He did not save the world, but God destined him to play a role in the life of the incarnate Son. Joseph was to act as father to the holy child. *As father*, he was to protect and guide him. Since the Church is the body of Christ, it can be understood as a continuation of the Incarnation. Accordingly, the Church teaches that Joseph's fatherly care for the incarnate Christ continues, only now it extends to his body, the Church.

Joseph now has a twofold role in the Church. First, he intercedes. Just as he protected the Holy Family during his earthly life, he now protects the Church *through his powerful intercession*. Since the time of Leo XIII, the Church has officially implored the protection of Saint Joseph (*RC* 30) and, as John Paul II adds, has done so particularly for families, which are a foundational cell of the Church and of society. Second, after Mary, Joseph serves as the model of *how to cooperate* with the process of salvation. He was faithful, had a pure heart, walked in holiness, was just, and obeyed the word of God (*RC* 31). These virtues are necessary if we are to arrive at the fullness of salvation. Thus Saint Joseph is a model of these virtues and of how to walk in the way of salvation. With good reason, then, he is patron of the universal Church, and he is also a patron for each of us personally on our pilgrimage.

1. The Church sees in Saint Joseph a man who exercised fatherly care over Jesus and who now continues that same fatherly care for the Church, which is the body of his reputed Son. Do I recognize or think of Saint Joseph as having fatherly care for me and my family and our concerns?

2. The Church considers herself a body composed of many people who in Christ are organically connected to each other. We profoundly affect and help one another. This apostolic exhortation encourages us to ask Saint Joseph for his prayers because he is such a powerful intercessor. As he cared for Christ, so his fatherly care continues for those who are members of Christ. Do I try to live my life by myself, relying mainly on my own strength? How can I begin living more *corporately*, seeing myself as a part of the body of Christ? How can I allow Saint Joseph and other saints to help me by their prayers?

Pray

Saint Joseph, thank you for obeying God's word to you and for acting as the earthly father of Jesus. Enfold me and my family into your heart. Keep praying for us and all our needs, until we attain the fullness of salvation. Amen.

Act

We all carry many personal and family burdens. Find time to be quiet and ask Saint Joseph to intercede for each person you hold in your heart. Naming each one, ask Saint Joseph to carry that person in his heart and to pray for the need until it is resolved.

Notes

1. Cf. Saint Irenaeus, *Adversus Haereses*, IV, 23, 1: S. Ch. 100/2, 692–694.

2. Leo XIII, Encyclical Epistle *Quamquam Pluries* (August 15, 1889): *Leonis XIII PM Acta*, IX (1890), 175–182.

3. Sacred Congregation of Rites, Decree *Quemadmodum Deus* (December 8, 1870): *Pii IX P.M Acta*, pars I, vol. V, 282; Pius IX, Apostolic Letter *Inclytum Patriarcham* (July 7, 1871): loc. cit., 331–335.

4. Cf. Saint John Chrysostom, *In Matth. Hom.* V, 3: *PG* 57, 57f. The Fathers of the Church and the Popes, on the basis of their common name, also saw in Joseph of Egypt a prototype of Joseph of Nazareth, inasmuch as the former foreshadowed in some way the ministry and greatness of the latter, who was guardian of God the Father's most precious treasures—the Incarnate Word and his most holy Mother: cf., for example, Saint Bernard, *Super "Missus est,"* Hom. II, 16: *S. Bernardi Opera*, Ed. Cist., IV, 33f.; Leo XIII, Encyclical Epistle *Quamquam Pluries*, loc. cit., 179.

5. Second Vatican Ecumenical Council, Dogmatic Constitution on the Church *Lumen Gentium*, 58.

6. Cf. ibid., 63.

7. Second Vatican Ecumenical Council, Dogmatic Constitution on Divine Revelation *Dei Verbum*, 5.

8. Ibid., 2.

9. Cf. *Lumen Gentium*, 63.

10. *Dei Verbum*, 2.

11. Sacred Congregation of Rites, Decree *Novis hisce temporibus* (November 13, 1962): *AAS* 54 (1962), 873. [On May 1, 2013, Joseph's name was also added to Eucharistic Prayers II, III, and IV with the approval of Pope Francis. *Ed.*]

12. Saint Augustine, *Sermo* 51, 10, 16: *PL* 38, 342.

13. Saint Augustine, *De nuptiis et concupiscentia*, I, 11, 12: *PL* 44, 421; cf. *De consensu evangelistarum*, II, 1, 2: PL 34, 1071; *Contra Faustum*, III 2: *PL* 42. 214.

14. Saint Augustine, *De nuptiis et concupiscentia*, I, 11, 13: *PL* 44, 421; cf. *Contra Iulianum*, V, 12, 46: *PL* 44, 810.

15. Cf. Saint Augustine, *Contra Faustum*, XXIII, 8: *PL* 42, 470f.; *De consensu evangelistarum*, II, 1, 3: *PL* 34, 1072; *Sermo*, 51, 13, 21: *PL* 38, 344f.; Saint Thomas, *Summa Theol.*, III, q. 29, a. 2 in conclus.

16. Cf. *Discourses* of January 9, 16, February 20, 1980: *Insegnamenti*, III/I (1980), pp. 88–92; 148–152; 428–431.

17. Paul VI, *Discourse* to the "Equipes Notre-Dame" Movement (May 4, 1970). n. 7: *AAS* 62, (1970), 431. Similar praise of the Family of Nazareth as a perfect example of domestic life can be found, for example, in Leo XIII, Apostolic Letter *Neminem Fugit* (June 14, 1892); *Leonis XIII PM Acta*, XII (1892), 149f.; Benedict XV, *Motu Proprio Bonum Sane* (July 25, 1920): *AAS* 12 (1920), 313–317.

18. Apostolic Exhortation *Familiaris Consortio* (November 22, 1981), 17: *AAS* 74 (1982), 100.

19. Ibid., 49: loc. cit., 140; cf. *Lumen Gentium*, 11; Decree on the Apostolate of the Laity, *Apostolicam Actuositatem*, 11.

20. *Familiaris Consortio*, 85: loc. cit., 189f.

21. Cf. Saint John Chrysostom, *In Matth. Hom.*, V, 3: *PG* 57, 57f.

22. Paul VI, *Discourse* (March 19, 1966): *Insegnamenti, IV* (1966), 110.

23. Cf. *Roman Missal*, Collect for the Solemnity of Saint Joseph, Husband of the Blessed Virgin Mary.

24. Cf. ibid., Preface for the Solemnity of Saint Joseph, Husband of the Blessed Virgin Mary.

25. Leo XIII, *Quamquam Pluries*, loc. cit., 178.

26. Pius XII, Radio Message to Catholic School Students in the United States of America (February 19, 1958): *AAS* 50 (1958), 174.

27. Origen, *Hom. XIII in Lucam*, 7: S. Ch. 87, 214f.

28. Origen, *Hom. XI in Lucam*, 6: S. Ch. 87, 196f.

29. Cf. Roman Missal, *Eucharistic Prayer* 1.

30. Sacred Congregation of Rites, Decree *Quemadmodum Deus*, loc. cit., p. 282.

31. *Collection of Masses of the Blessed Virgin Mary*, I, "Our Lady of Nazareth," Preface.

32. *Familiaris Consortio*, 16.

33. Leo XIII, *Quamquam Pluries*, loc. cit., 177f.

34. Cf. Encyclical Letter *Laborem Exercens* (September 14, 1981), 9: *AAS* 73 (1981), 599ff.

35. Ibid., 24: loc. cit., p. 638. The Popes in recent times have constantly presented Saint Joseph as the "model" of workers and laborers; see, for example, Leo XIII, *Quamquam pluries*, loc. cit., 180; Benedict XV, *Motu Proprio Bonum Sane*, loc. cit. 314–316; Pius XII, *Discourse* (March 11, 1945), 4: *AAS* 37 (1945), 72; *Discourse* (May 1 1955): *AAS* 47 (1955), 406; John XXIII, *Radio Address* (May 1, 1960): *AAS* 52 (1960), 398.

36. Paul VI, *Discourse* (March 19, 1969): *Insegnamenti*, VII (1969), 1268.

37. Ibid., loc. cit., 1267.

38. Cf. Saint Thomas, *Summa Theol.* II–II, q. 82, a. 3, ad 2.

39. Ibid., III q. 8, a. 1, ad 1.

40. Cf. Pius XII. Encyclical Letter *Haurietis Aquas* (May 15, 1956), III *AAS* 48 (1956), 329f.

41. Cf. Saint Thomas, *Summa Theol.* II–II, q. 182, a. 1, ad 3.

42. Cf. Sacred Congregation of Rites, *Quemadmodum Deus*, loc. cit., 283.

43. Ibid., loc. cit., 282f.

44. Leo XIII, *Quamquam Pluries*, loc. cit., 177–179.

45. Post-Synodal Apostolic Exhortation *Christifideles Laici* (December 30, 1988), 34: *AAS* 81 (1989), 456.

46. *Dei Verbum*, 1.

47. Paul VI, *Discourse* (March 19, 1969): *Insegnamenti*, VII (1969), 1269.

48. Cf. *Roman Missal*, Collect, Prayer over the Gifts for the Solemnity of Saint Joseph, Husband of the Blessed Virgin Mary; Prayer after Communion from the Votive Mass of Saint Joseph.

49. Cf. Leo XII, "Oratio ad Sanctum Iosephum," contained immediately after the text of the Encyclical Epistle *Quamquam Pluries, Leonis XIII PM. Acta*, IX (1890), 183.

50. Sacred Congregation of Rites, *Quemadmodum Deus*, loc. cit., 282.

JOSEPH C. ATKINSON, PHD, is a leading expert in the theology of the domestic church. He is the author of *The Biblical and Theological Foundations of the Family* (The Catholic University of America Press, 2013) and founder of the Theology of the Family Project (theologyofthefamily.com). In 2007, EWTN produced a thirteen-part series with Dr. Atkinson entitled *The Biblical Vision of Marriage and Family: The Domestic Church.* Currently the Associate Professor of Sacred Scripture at the John Paul II Institute at The Catholic University of America in Washington, D.C., Dr. Atkinson also serves as executive secretary of the Catholic Biblical Association. He and his wife have been married thirty-three years and have six children and one grandchild.

MORE TITLES IN THE SERIES

Mother of the Redeemer
Anniversary Edition
Redemptoris Mater

Written by John Paul II with commentary
by M. Jean Frisk

Commemorate the 25th Anniversary of John Paul II's encyclical
Mother of the Redeemer with a rich commentary presenting Mary as
a model of faith.

Paperback   128 pages
0-8198-4902-2 $8.95 U.S.

On the Dignity and Vocation of Women
Anniversary Edition
Mulieris Dignitatem

Written by John Paul II with commentary
by Genevieve Kineke

This annotated edition of Pope John Paul II's apostolic letter
responds to urgent questions raised in recent decades about the
role and value of women.

Paperback   160 pages
0-8198-5455-7 $8.95 U.S.

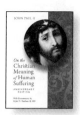

On the Christian Meaning of Human Suffering Anniverary Edition
Salvifici Doloris

Written by John Paul II with commentary by Myles N. Sheehan, SJ, MD

This 30th anniversary edition features the complete text of the letter plus commentary by a priest and physician trained in geriatrics with an expertise in palliative care.

Paperback   128 pages
0-8198-5458-1 $8.95 U.S.

BOOKS & MEDIA

A mission of the Daughters of St. Paul

As apostles of Jesus Christ, evangelizing today's world:

We are CALLED to holiness
by God's living Word and Eucharist.

We COMMUNICATE the Gospel message
through our lives and through all
available forms of media.

We SERVE the Church
by responding to the hopes and needs
of all people with the Word of God,
in the spirit of St. Paul.

For more information visit our website: www.pauline.org.

BOOKS & MEDIA

The Daughters of St. Paul operate book and media centers at the following addresses. Visit, call or write the one nearest you today, or find us at www.pauline.org.

CALIFORNIA

3908 Sepulveda Blvd, Culver City, CA 90230	310-397-8676
935 Brewster Avenue, Redwood City, CA 94063	650-369-4230
5945 Balboa Avenue, San Diego, CA 92111	858-565-9181

FLORIDA

145 S.W. 107th Avenue, Miami, FL 33174	305-559-6715

HAWAII

1143 Bishop Street, Honolulu, HI 96813	808-521-2731
Neighbor Islands call:	866-521-2731

ILLINOIS

172 North Michigan Avenue, Chicago, IL 60601	312-346-4228

LOUISIANA

4403 Veterans Memorial Blvd, Metairie, LA 70006	504-887-7631

MASSACHUSETTS

885 Providence Hwy, Dedham, MA 02026	781-326-5385

MISSOURI

9804 Watson Road, St. Louis, MO 63126	314-965-3512

NEW YORK

64 W. 38th Street, New York, NY 10018	212-754-1110

PENNSYLVANIA

Philadelphia—relocating	215-676-9494

SOUTH CAROLINA

243 King Street, Charleston, SC 29401	843-577-0175

VIRGINIA

1025 King Street, Alexandria, VA 22314	703-549-3806

CANADA

3022 Dufferin Street, Toronto, ON M6B 3T5	416-781-9131

¡También somos su fuente para libros,
videos y música en español!